Girls desire to know that they are beautiful and special. In a ~~~~~~~~ ~~ ~ outward beauty is adored and applauded on social ~~~~~~~~~~~~~~ help our daughters build their self-worth on God ~~~~~~~~~~~ ring my daughter's formative years whilst she was ~~~~~~

Through her finely crafted words, Sanc ~~~~~~~~~~ ..iu daughters by the hand and awakens the truths in Psaln ~~~~~~ ji. building foundational biblical truths, she helps the reader craft beautiful and lasting heart-connection mother-daughter relationships. This book needs to be lovingly pressed into the hand of every mother who is raising a daughter.

—Heidi McLaughlin

International speaker and author of *Fresh Joy: Finding Joy in the Midst of Loss, Hardship and Suffering* (Castle Quay Books)

Mother-daughter relationships, I know from experience, are not always natural treasures. My mother and I wrestled spiritually and relationally most of her life. So I was intrigued many years ago when Sandee's mother, Gloria, after her own mom's passing, said, "She left us a wonderful legacy." Through Gloria's leadership of our church women's group, a godly heritage was richly evident, and Sandee was a delight as our son's senior kindergarten teacher. No wonder my friend Sandee's passion for years has been encouraging moms and their daughters to build a bond of trust as they grow in God's word together. An antidote to typical distancing through the teen years, this shared journey will help mother and daughter build a solid foundation for life in an increasingly individualistic and uncertain world!

—Moira Brown

Broadcaster, author, former co-host of *100 Huntley Street*

Psalm 119 is my favourite psalm; it is rich in the attributes of God and what it means to be walking with the Almighty at your side. Psalm 119 is full of practical living for an abundant life.

It takes true focus and tools like this fantastic study by Sandee Macgregor to grow our daughters into the richness of a relationship with God. Spiritual parenting takes deliberate work, relationship, and solid biblical teaching, and I highly recommend this devotional tool for that important journey of raising your daughter to know her Saviour. What a precious gift this book will be to your mother-daughter relationship, and in your relationship with God.

—Lorna Dueck

Retired CEO of Crossroads Christian Communications, journalist, and columnist

Sandee Macgregor has written a devotional that helps strengthen you and your daughter's relationship with God and each another. Based on Psalm 119, thoughtful sections help ignite discussion and encourage prayer and memorization, while fostering a deep sense of connection with one another. A journal section is also included for much needed mutual encouragement, along with suggested activities to enjoy together. Sandee's devotional is an inspiring resource, one that will bolster and enliven not only your daughter's faith but also your own.

—Melanie Stevenson

Author of *One More Tomorrow* and *Soul Focus—Trials*, speaker, and blogger at www. scentofheaven.me

Being parents of four children, including two preteen girls, we are delighted and thankful for this excellent devotional by Sandee Macgregor. This is a resource packed with truth and yet easy to access through practical prompts and application in the study of God's word. In a day when our young people are so often confused and misled, this book powerfully instills life-changing wisdom and clarity from Psalm 119.

There is a serious battle raging for the hearts and minds of young girls right now and that is why we are excited to use this within our own family and to wholeheartedly recommend it to others.

—Robbie and Gillian Symons

Senior pastor and pastor's wife of Hope Bible Church, Oakville

A devotional that unfolds like a treasure-seeking journey—beautifully written and overflowing with love for God and a deep reverence for his word. A guide for all mothers who long to walk with their daughters along this path, straight to the feet of Jesus. New treasures as well as old are found, polished, and displayed in all their radiance.

—Lori McAuley

Health care coordinator at Muskoka Woods Sports Resort

Sandee Macgregor

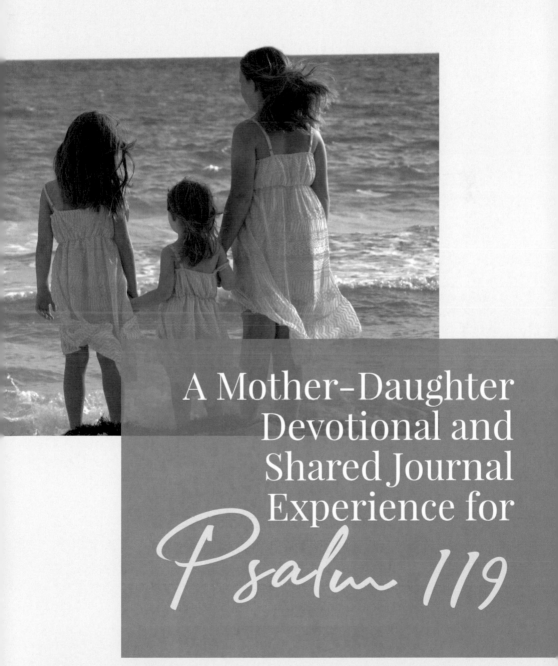

A Mother–Daughter
Devotional and
Shared Journal
Experience for
Psalm 119

A MOTHER-DAUGHTER DEVOTIONAL AND SHARED JOURNAL
EXPERIENCE FOR PSALM 119
Copyright ©2021 Sandee Macgregor
All rights reserved
ISBN 978-1-988928-41-8 Soft Cover
ISBN 978-1-988928-42-5 EPUB

Published by: Castle Quay Books
Burlington, ON, Canada | Jupiter, FL, USA
Tel: (416) 573-3249
E-mail: info@castlequaybooks.com | www.castlequaybooks.com

Edited by Marina Hofman Willard
Cover design and journal concept by Imprint Marketing Group Inc.
Book interior by Burst Impressions
Printed in Canada

Library and Archives Canada Cataloguing in Publication
\Title: A mother-daughter devotional and shared journal experience for Psalm 119 / by
Sandee G Macgregor.
Names: Macgregor, Sandee G., author.
Identifiers: Canadiana 2020034465X | ISBN 9781988928418 (softcover)
Subjects: LCSH: Bible. Psalms—Meditations. | LCSH: Bible. Psalms—Devotional
literature. | LCSH: Daughters—Religious life. | LCSH: Mothers—Religious life. | LCSH:
Mothers and daughters—Religious aspects—Christianity. | LCSH: Spiritual journals—
Authorship.
Classification: LCC BS1430.54 .M33 2020 | DDC 242/.62—dc23

CASTLE QUAY BOOKS

For my mom, my strength and steady.

Early in life, my mother taught me about God's love and connected me to the gospel. Her life has always reflected that the Bible is truth and enriches all aspects of my journey.

I come from a legacy of God-fearing women—my grandmothers, Nellie and Frieda, and my mother, Gloria: This is dedicated to you with a prayer that I will do for my daughters what you have done for me.

Mom, I love you and I thank you. May the Lord unfold your words to the next generation (Psalm 119:130).

Sandee Macgregor

 is the creator and founder of the website Sovereign Radiance, a hope-filled place for mothers to be encouraged with the truth of the gospel while they are reminded that they are not alone in their journey. Educated and trained as a teacher, Sandee continues to teach at home while pursuing her love of writing. She is a follower of Christ, wife to Duncan for 25 years, and a mom to 5 children. To learn more about Sandee and to follow her on the journey into the heart of motherhood, visit her blog at www.sovereignradiance.com.

Contents

Acknowledgements

To the team at Imprint Marketing Group—Halcyon, Janice, and Meg: Your creative genius brought to life my vision for blogging at Sovereign Radiance and this devotional that God placed on my heart. My gratitude is overflowing.

To the beautiful ones who prayerfully helped me process my thoughts—Mom, Charmaine, Paula, Moira, Stef, and Erin: You provided a safe place and gave me unique insights to keep me moving forward. Dad, your love and prayers carry me always. John, thank you for timely advice and encouragement.

To Larry, Marina, and the team at Castle Quay Books: Thank you for believing in this project. It is an honour to work together and watch this unfold.

To my husband, Duncan: Thank you for the endless love and encouragement. You listened to my many ramblings and read through multiple copies with patience. I love you.

To my daughters—Samantha, Sara, and Katie: This was inspired by you and is for you. Thank you for being the first ones to go through the early beginnings of this devotional. May the legacy continue.

To my sons—Chris and Jack: The support you provide does not go unnoticed. Thank you for telling me to stop being afraid and just do it! Lord willing, the next devotional will be for mothers and sons, inspired by you. It is in the works!

To my heavenly Father: "May these words of my mouth and this meditation of my heart be pleasing in your sight, LORD, my Rock and my Redeemer" (Psalm 19:14).

From My Mom, Gloria Mudge

I had a great mom, a mother in the truest sense of the word, who ingrained in her children a desire to serve the Lord. She left us a wonderful legacy. The essence of her life was giving to others, and she passed it on to her children, who have passed it on to their children. She was a model and influence in the way she lived her life before us, through her lovely smile and her constant love and devotion to her husband and to the Lord. She was a teacher who taught and trained us in the ways of the Lord. Her prayers and her hospitality positively affected our lives, and the richness of her spirituality is a treasure stored up in Heaven.

Sandee has drawn from her deep springs of recall. I see in her the fulfillment of years of writing down life-given and God-given promptings, and she is now using these tools to hand off a guide to fellow moms and the next generation. Commitment and love from a mom who knows her daughter's heart.

Gloria

To Mothers

Dear Mothers,

In these fast-paced, challenging days, your daughter's heart is being pulled in many different directions. Being present in her life allows you to nurture your God-given mother-daughter relationship. Engaging with her in all areas of her life will strengthen your connection, deepen your bond, and build a foundation for years to come.

Remember that you are not alone on this journey of motherhood—God is with you every step of the way and has given all you need through his word. As Hebrews 4:16 says, "Let us then approach God's throne of grace with confidence, so that we may receive mercy and find grace to help us in our time of need." It is possible to point your daughter to Christ with your gaze fixed on Jesus so you can radiate his lavish love: "Those who look to him are radiant; their faces are never covered with shame" (Psalm 34:5).

If there ever was a time to encourage the heart of your daughter to draw closer to God, it is now! May God's word unfold into your relationship and be your source of daily strength and joy as you study Psalm 119 together, one verse at a time.

"The unfolding of your words gives light."
Psalm 119:130

Using this Devotional and Journal

Each week begins with a Dear Moms section that is a special encouragement for you. After reading your "Mom" devotional, spend time with your daughter experiencing the Conversations and Connections interactive devotional together. Scriptures are provided for you in the NIV translation; consider examining other translations of Psalm 119 to gain a deeper knowledge of the passages. Allow for extra time on each day 5 for Dear Moments. Here, you will write notes of encouragement to others and do an activity together.

Then, turn to the journal section at the back of this book. In the Shared Journal Experience, called *the switch* by my youngest daughter, you are invited to connect with your daughter by switching back and forth, writing encouraging words of love and Scripture to one another. Inspired by my mother's tradition of leaving encouraging notes for her children, with God's blessing, I encourage mothers and daughters to write to each other regularly.

Taking time to think through our words allows us to communicate thoughtfully and creatively and present a unique way to inspire the hearts of our loved ones. Words are the vessel the Lord has chosen to speak to us. The time it takes to write a simple note is worth the encouragement your daughter will receive.

When the journal is complete, look back and discover what you have learned together. In the years to come, may this journal provide you with memorable words to reflect on with gratitude.

I pray that this devotional and journal will create many meaningful moments for you and your daughter and that you will cherish this written record of your hope-filled journey through Psalm 119 together.

Go ahead, write a word; inspire her heart!

Psalm 119
Devotional

Practicing His Presence

Psalm 119:1-40
Let your strength come from the Lord as you rest in his presence.

Memory Verse
"Open my eyes that I may see wonderful things in your law."
Psalm 119:18

Dear Moms

A chosen few purple jackets graced the hallways of a small Canadian conservative school over sixty years ago. They were worn by a group of girls who wanted to set themselves apart by dressing alike. They wanted to feel unique but have a sense of solidarity and security, that they belonged together. How long the purple jacket fad lasted remains only in the memories of the girls who wore them, but the idea of intentionally creating a sense of belonging has far outlasted the fashion statement. I wish I could have known my mom when she was proudly wearing the purple jacket!

Isaiah 43:1 reveals how personal God is and that we belong to him: "But now, this is what the Lord says—he who created you, Jacob, he who formed you, Israel: 'Do not fear, for I have redeemed you; I have summoned you by name; you are mine.'" How wonderful it is to know that he has called us by name and we are his! The question of belonging can linger and create anxiety if we forget the promise of this beautiful passage. In 1 John 3:1, we are reminded of God's love: "See what great love the Father has lavished on us, that we should be called children of God! And that is what we are!" We have an opportunity to be in relationship with a personal, loving God. We don't need a "purple jacket" to fill the need to belong; we need

Jesus! If he is missing in our lives, we try to fill our need to belong elsewhere and miss practicing the presence of God.

Belonging is our first felt need as human beings, and this desire continues to permeate our world and communities. This thought lingers in the soul of our precious daughters, regardless of whether they experience belonging in a particular friend group, team, family, or church. What if we could take the sense of belonging and wrap it up as a beautiful gift with a personalized invitation inscribed on it? It might read,

Dear daughter, you are a child of God and are invited to belong to your heavenly Father. He created you, loves you, and has a plan for you. You belong to him, beautiful one.

I love how God reminds us of this truth in Isaiah: "For I am the LORD your God who takes hold of your right hand ... I, the LORD, have called you in righteousness; I will take hold of your hand. I will keep you" (41:13; 42:6). Our daughters are a gift on loan to us from God, the Creator and Sustainer of life. As mothers we are called to remind them that they are deeply loved by us, and even more by our Redeemer.

To be in community sharing, giving, and loving is how we are wired. As Christ-followers, regardless of whether we are more introverted or extroverted, we have a choice of how we fulfill this longing to belong. It may be in ways that are very quiet or very loud, but it is there. Motherhood allows us the opportunity to gently guide our daughters to practice his presence and to gift them with a better understanding that they belong to God.

Perhaps you had a jacket of a different colour while walking your hallways of life. Your daughter will too. Let's help her wear the well-worn truths of God's word, and let that be the fabric of her identity.

Conversations and Connections with Your Daughter

WEEK 1

Day 1

Read through Psalm 119:1–8.

א Aleph[1]
¹ Blessed are those whose ways are blameless,
who walk according to the law of the LORD.
² Blessed are those who keep his statutes
and seek him with all their heart—
³ they do no wrong
but follow his ways.
⁴ You have laid down precepts
that are to be fully obeyed.
⁵ Oh, that my ways were steadfast
in obeying your decrees!
⁶ Then I would not be put to shame
when I consider all your commands.
⁷ I will praise you with an upright heart
as I learn your righteous laws.
⁸ I will obey your decrees;
do not utterly forsake me.

Highlight words or phrases that create a sense of how you can practice the presence of God. Discuss the phrases *blessed, blameless, walk according to the law, statutes, follow his ways, fully obeyed, steadfast,* and *praise.* What do these phrases mean for your daily walk with God? Consider the ways in which your life is a testimony that reveals Christ to others.

Today's Key Verse

"Blessed are those who keep his statutes and seek him with all their heart" (Psalm 119:2).

Pray Together

Pray for God to help you walk in obedience and reflect Christ to others.

---

1. Psalm 119 is an "acrostic" poem divided into 22 sections that each begin with a letter of the Hebrew alphabet.

Memorize the Weekly Verse

"Open my eyes that I may see wonderful things in your law" (Psalm 119:18).

Shared Journal Experience

Turn to the journal section for week 1, day 1, in this book and switch back and forth to share words of encouragement to one another.

Day 2

Read Psalm 119:9–16.

ב Beth

[9] How can a young person stay on the path of purity?
By living according to your word.
[10] I seek you with all my heart;
do not let me stray from your commands.
[11] I have hidden your word in my heart
that I might not sin against you.
[12] Praise be to you, LORD;
teach me your decrees.
[13] With my lips I recount
all the laws that come from your mouth.
[14] I rejoice in following your statutes
as one rejoices in great riches.
[15] I meditate on your precepts
and consider your ways.
[16] I delight in your decrees;
I will not neglect your word.

Highlight words or phrases that create a sense of how you can practice the presence of God. Discuss the phrases *path, purity, living according to your word, seek, heart, stray, hidden your word, rejoice, meditate,* and *not neglect your word*. What do these phrases mean for your daily walk with God? Consider the ways that your heart can become distracted.

Today's Key Verse

"I have hidden your word in my heart that I might not sin against you" (Psalm 119:11).

Pray Together

Pray that your hearts will not be easily distracted.

Memorize the Weekly Verse

"Open my eyes that I may see wonderful things in your law" (Psalm 119:18).

Shared Journal Experience

Turn to the journal section for week 1, day 2, and switch back and forth to share words of encouragement to one another.

Day 3

Read Psalm 119:17–24.

ג Gimel

¹⁷ Be good to your servant while I live,
that I may obey your word.
¹⁸ Open my eyes that I may see
wonderful things in your law.
¹⁹ I am a stranger on earth;
do not hide your commands from me.
²⁰ My soul is consumed with longing
for your laws at all times.
²¹ You rebuke the arrogant, who are accursed,
those who stray from your commands.
²² Remove from me their scorn and contempt,
for I keep your statutes.
²³ Though rulers sit together and slander me,
your servant will meditate on your decrees.
²⁴ Your statutes are my delight;
they are my counselors.

Highlight words or phrases that create a sense of how you can practice the presence of God. Discuss the phrases *servant, obey your word, open my eyes, wonderful things, stranger on earth, longing for your laws,* and *your servant.* What do these phrases mean for your daily walk with God? Consider the ways you can obey God's word.

Today's Key Verse

"Your statutes are my delight; they are my counselors" (Psalm 119:24).

Pray Together

Pray for a willingness to obey God's word and see wonderful things in his law.

Memorize the Weekly Verse

"Open my eyes that I may see wonderful things in your law" (Psalm 119:18).

Shared Journal Experience

Turn to the journal section for week 1, day 3, and switch back and forth, sharing words of encouragement.

Read Psalm 119:25–32.

ד Daleth

²⁵ I am laid low in the dust;
preserve my life according to your word.
²⁶ I gave an account of my ways and you answered me;
teach me your decrees.
²⁷ Cause me to understand the way of your precepts,
that I may meditate on your wonderful deeds.
²⁰ My soul is weary with sorrow;
strengthen me according to your word.
²⁹ Keep me from deceitful ways;
be gracious to me and teach me your law.
³⁰ I have chosen the way of faithfulness;
I have set my heart on your laws.
³¹ I hold fast to your statutes, LORD;
do not let me be put to shame.
³² I run in the path of your commands,
for you have broadened my understanding.

Highlight words or phrases that create a sense of how you can practice the presence of God. Discuss the phrases *account, teach me your decrees, understand, precepts, strengthen, gracious, chosen, faithfulness, set my heart, hold fast,* and *run in the path*. What do these phrases mean for your daily walk with God? Consider the ways you sometimes run away from God's commandments.

Today's Key Verse

"I run in the path of your commands, for you have broadened my understanding" (Psalm 119:32).

Pray Together

Pray that you would understand and follow God's commandments.

Memorize the Weekly Verse

"Open my eyes that I may see wonderful things in your law" (Psalm 119:18).

Shared Journal Experience

Turn to the journal section for week 1, day 4, and switch back and forth, sharing words of encouragement.

Day 5

Read Psalm 119:33–40.

ה He

³³ Teach me, LORD, the way of your decrees,
that I may follow it to the end.
³⁴ Give me understanding, so that I may keep your law
and obey it with all my heart.
³⁵ Direct me in the path of your commands,
for there I find delight.
³⁶ Turn my heart toward your statutes
and not toward selfish gain.
³⁷ Turn my eyes away from worthless things;
preserve my life according to your word.
³⁸ Fulfill your promise to your servant,
so that you may be feared.
³⁹ Take away the disgrace I dread,
for your laws are good.
⁴⁰ How I long for your precepts!
In your righteousness preserve my life.

Highlight words or phrases that create a sense of how you can practice the presence of God. Discuss the phrases *teach, give me understanding, obey, direct me, turn my heart, according to your word, your laws are good*, and *righteousness*. What do these phrases mean to your daily walk with God? Consider the ways you can turn your heart to God.

Today's Key Verse

"Turn my heart toward your statutes and not toward selfish gain" (Psalm 119:36).

Pray Together

Pray that you would turn your heart toward God and not to worthless things.

Memorize the Weekly Verse

"Open my eyes that I may see wonderful things in your law" (Psalm 119:18).

Shared Journal Experience

Turn to the journal section for week 1, day 5, and switch back and forth, sharing words of encouragement.

Dear Moments Together

Today, write a note to a family member to encourage them with a verse from Psalm 119 and remind them that they are loved by God (such as Psalm 119:26, 46, 64).

Trace your daughter's feet and cut them out. Write on or attach the key verse to the cut-outs. Have fun placing the feet on the ground in the correct order and saying the verse out loud as you walk on them.

Worship together with these songs as you reflect on God's presence in your life.

"King of Kings" (Hillsong Worship)

"Till I Found You" (Phil Wickham)

"Now I Belong" (Hope Kids Worship, featuring Kenzie Cline)

"No Longer Slaves" (Zach Williams)

Closing Prayer for Week 1

Dear Lord, thank you for this time together with my daughter. It is a gift to walk with her through the verses of Psalm 119. Guide us, Lord, as we seek to practice your presence every day. Reveal to us by your Holy Spirit all the ways to prayerfully praise you. May we truly know how to belong to you first. With our whole hearts we want to seek you, move toward your word, and not wander away. May we be diligent to store your word in our hearts and practice your presence. Amen.

WEEK 2
Seeking Truth, Speaking Truth

Psalm 119:41-80

Be the one who speaks truth once it's found.

Memory Verse

"Never take your word of truth from my mouth,
for I have put my hope in your law."
Psalm 119:43

Dear Moms

Leaving the comforts of home is challenging. After my parents told us we were leaving our west coast home for Ontario, I felt like the familiar frame that had enclosed my life up to that point had broken, and I wondered if it would ever be the same again. I had to face a new school, home, church, and friend group all at once. It became very real once the station wagon was packed and we were speeding down the Trans-Canada highway, eastbound towards the great unknown.

I put my hope in what I would meet at the end of that journey. I trusted the wisdom of my parents and that we would be okay in our new life. My parents in turn trusted that God was in control. I watched them fulfill the calm pursuit of a calling to move their family across the country, and I rested in that truth.

Knowing from an early age that God was in control saved me from many paths of potential destruction. My parents taught me to trust them and, ultimately, to trust my heavenly Father. As mothers, the gift we have been given is the ability to teach biblical truth early on so that our daughters can quickly learn to discern when the enemy whispers lies. At first glance it may seem simple, but the enemy seeks to draw a line so faint that a lie can easily masquerade as the truth. John 8:44 says, "he is a liar and the father of lies."

Have you ever believed a lie so deeply that the truth just did not resonate and it seemed impossible to see and hear the difference? This has happened to me many times. Times where I allowed the truth of various situations to be uprooted, so that a lie was able to plant itself in its place. My mind was full of doubt: Am I good enough? Am I capable? Am I worthy?

It's not a question of *if* your daughter will ask herself these questions, but *when*. Think of a time when you were young, and share with her a moment when a lie burst forth and you succumbed to its grip. What did you do about it? What was the outcome? Share how you have experienced that now, as an adult, and what you do to overcome the lie with truth. Ask your daughter to share a lie that lingers and a time when she felt that telling a lie was easier than speaking the truth.

Forgiveness and confession are beautiful ways to heal from the poor choices we have made. James 5:16 reminds us, "Therefore, confess your sins to each other and pray for each other so that you may be healed." It's hard to confess, but freedom comes when we act. The truth we can share with our daughters comes from our mistakes and the grace that we have been shown through Jesus.

Although moving was not a choice that I actively made, it was something that God invited me to do—a journey of faith to undertake with my family. When we arrived at our new home after driving across a large expanse of the country with six people in tow, the orange carpet in the new house along with the bedroom I claimed (with the big closet!) became a comfort to me. In truth, I was scared. I had begun the practice of watching my parents place their trust in God, as I had placed my own in them. This ended up being a foundational part of how I sought truth amidst the lies and spoke it to a new part of my life.

Conversations and Connections with Your Daughter

WEEK 2

Day 1

Read Psalm 119:41–48.

٦ Waw

41 May your unfailing love come to me, LORD,
your salvation, according to your promise;
42 then I can answer anyone who taunts me,
for I trust in your word.
43 Never take your word of truth from my mouth,
for I have put my hope in your laws.
44 I will always obey your law,
for ever and ever.
45 I will walk about in freedom,
for I have sought out your precepts.
46 I will speak of your statutes before kings
and will not be put to shame,
47 for I delight in your commands
because I love them.
48 I reach out for your commands, which I love,
that I may meditate on your decrees.

Highlight words or phrases that create a sense of how you can seek truth and speak truth. Discuss the phrases *unfailing love, salvation, promise, trust, hope, obey, I will walk, freedom, speak of your statutes,* and *meditate on your decrees.* What do these phrases mean for your daily walk with God? Consider ways to walk in freedom.

Today's Key Verse

"I will walk about in freedom, for I have sought out your precepts" (Psalm 119:45).

Pray Together

Pray for God to help you to walk in freedom and seek him.

Memorize the Weekly Verse

"Never take your word of truth from my mouth, for I have put my hope in your law" (Psalm 119:43).

Shared Journal Experience

Turn to the journal section for week 2, day 1, and switch back and forth, sharing words of encouragement.

Day 2

Read Psalm 119:49–56.

ז Zayin

[49] Remember your word to your servant,
for you have given me hope.
[50] My comfort in my suffering is this:
Your promise preserves my life.
[51] The arrogant mock me unmercifully,
but I do not turn from your law.
[52] I remember, LORD, your ancient laws,
and I find comfort in them.
[53] Indignation grips me because of the wicked,
who have forsaken your law.
[54] Your decrees are the theme of my song
wherever I lodge.
[55] In the night, LORD, I remember your name,
that I may keep your law.
[56] This has been my practice:
I obey your precepts.

Highlight words or phrases that create a sense of how you can seek truth and speak truth. Discuss the phrases *remember, servant, hope, promise, preserves, I find comfort in them, decrees, theme of my song, keep your law,* and *practice*. What do these phrases mean for your daily walk with God? Consider the ways in which your life reveals God's truth.

Today's Key Verse

"Remember your word to your servant, for you have given me hope" (Psalm 119:49).

Pray Together

Pray for God to help you to walk in the truth of his word.

Memorize the Weekly Verse

"Never take your word of truth from my mouth, for I have put my hope in your law" (Psalm 119:43).

Shared Journal Experience

Turn to the journal section for week 2, day 2, and switch back and forth, sharing words of encouragement.

Read Psalm 119:57–64.

ח Heth

⁵⁷ You are my portion, LORD;
I have promised to obey your words.
⁵⁸ I have sought your face with all my heart;
be gracious to me according to your promise.
⁵⁹ I have considered my ways
and have turned my steps to your statutes.
⁶⁰ I will hasten and not delay
to obey your commands.
⁶¹ Though the wicked bind me with ropes,
I will not forget your law.
⁶² At midnight I rise to give you thanks
for your righteous laws.
⁶³ I am a friend to all who fear you,
to all who follow your precepts.
⁶⁴ The earth is filled with your love, LORD;
teach me your decrees.

Highlight words or phrases that create a sense of how you can seek truth and speak truth. Discuss the phrases *portion, promised to obey, gracious, turned my steps, I will hasten, give you thanks, righteous laws, friend,* and *your love.* What do these phrases mean for your daily walk with God? Consider ways that God has filled the earth with his love.

Today's Key Verse

"I am a friend to all who fear you, to all who follow your precepts" (Psalm 119:63).

Pray Together

Pray for ways you can share God's love with others.

Memorize the Weekly Verse

"Never take your word of truth from my mouth, for I have put my hope in your law" (Psalm 119:43).

Shared Journal Experience

Turn to the journal section for week 2, day 3, and switch back and forth, sharing words of encouragement.

Day 4

Read Psalm 119:65–72.

⛉ Teth

[65] Do good to your servant
according to your word, LORD.
[66] Teach me knowledge and good judgment,
for I trust your commands.
[67] Before I was afflicted I went astray,
but now I obey your word.
[68] You are good, and what you do is good;
teach me your decrees.
[69] Though the arrogant have smeared me with lies,
I keep your precepts with all my heart.
[70] Their hearts are callous and unfeeling,
but I delight in your law.
[71] It was good for me to be afflicted
so that I might learn your decrees.
[72] The law from your mouth is more precious to me
than thousands of pieces of silver and gold.

Highlight words or phrases that create a sense of how you can seek truth and speak truth. Discuss the phrases *servant, your word, knowledge, good judgment, astray, obey your word, with all my heart, delight in your law,* and *learn your decrees.* What do these phrases mean for your daily walk with God? Consider the ways God's laws are more precious than a thousand pieces of silver and gold.

Today's Key Verse

"The law from your mouth is more precious to me than thousands of pieces of silver and gold" (Psalm 119:72).

Pray Together

Pray that you would see that God's laws are more precious than earthly treasures.

Memorize the Weekly Verse

"Never take your word of truth from my mouth, for I have put my hope in your law" (Psalm 119:43).

Shared Journal Experience

Turn to the journal section for week 2, day 4, and switch back and forth, sharing words of encouragement.

Read Psalm 119:73–80.

י Yodh

⁷³ Your hands made me and formed me;
give me understanding to learn your commands.
⁷⁴ May those who fear you rejoice when they see me,
for I have put my hope in your word.
⁷⁵ I know, Lord, that your laws are righteous,
and that in faithfulness you have afflicted me.
⁷⁶ May your unfailing love be my comfort,
according to your promise to your servant.
⁷⁷ Let your compassion come to me that I may live,
for your law is my delight.
⁷⁸ May the arrogant be put to shame for wronging me without cause;
but I will meditate on your precepts.
⁷⁹ May those who fear you turn to me,
those who understand your statutes.
⁸⁰ May I wholeheartedly follow your decrees,
that I may not be put to shame.

Highlight words or phrases that create a sense of how you can seek truth and speak truth. Discuss the phrases *hands made me, understanding, learn your commands, rejoice, hope in your word, righteous, faithfulness, unfailing love, comfort, compassion, meditate,* and *wholeheartedly follow.* What do they mean to your daily walk with God? Discuss the truth of his unfailing love.

Today's Key Verse

"May your unfailing love be my comfort, according to your promise to your servant" (Psalm 119:76).

Pray Together

Pray that you would know the truth of God's unfailing love.

Memorize the Weekly Verse

"Never take your word of truth from my mouth, for I have put my hope in your law" (Psalm 119:43).

Shared Journal Experience

Turn to the journal section for week 2, day 5, and switch back and forth, sharing words of encouragement.

Dear Moments Together

Write a note to a friend (or more than one friend!) today with a truth about God, and tell them how much you appreciate their friendship. Together, go out and purchase chocolate coins as a treat and enjoy them together. Remind your daughter that God's word is even more precious than chocolate!

Worship together with these songs as you reflect on the truth of God's love in your life.

"Is He Worthy?" (Chris Tomlin, featuring Andrew Peterson)

"Speak Life" (Toby Mac)

"Voice of Truth" (Casting Crowns)

"Truth be Told" (Matthew West)

Closing Prayer for Week 2

Dear Lord, we delight in you and take comfort when we think of the truths in your word. We know your unfailing love will come to us according to your promise. Help us to remember your laws and find comfort in them. Show us how to detect lies and immediately replace them with truth from your word. May your statutes be our song. We know you are our portion, and we commit today to keep your words. Even though we do not know what tomorrow brings, help us to remember to seek truth from your word and speak truth to others and ourselves. Thank you for your truth today. Amen.

WEEK 3
Abiding in Him

Psalm 119:81–120

Our moments and days are not determined by a finite line but by an eternal God with an infinite plan.

Memory Verse

"Your word is a lamp for my feet, a light on my path."
Psalm 119:105

Dear Moms

Rest is a precious desired gift. Often, we feel like we just can't get enough of it! Rest can mean different things for different people: walking, reading, working outside, coffee with a friend, or literally physically resting with a good nap.

I think of moments when I would drive to my sister's house with a car full of kids just bursting with energy and excitement to see their cousins while I was looking for the nearest bed to collapse on. Just for 15 minutes, I needed rest! Though I was exhausted, my own needs came second to those of my children.

Spiritually, if we are going to rest in God throughout our day, we need to learn to abide. Abiding is a choice we make to remain fixed on God. Through the verses of Psalm 119, we behold words and phrases that guide us towards a place of abiding, such as *delight, meditate, long, incline, turn our eyes, trust, and keep.* In verse 97, the psalmist invites us to a place where we can quietly sit at his feet: "Oh, how I love your law! I meditate on it all day long." The youthful exuberance of our daughters may cause us to believe that they don't need rest. If left unchecked, this may lead them later in life to devalue the importance of taking time to rest so that they can reflect upon their lives and grow in the knowledge of Jesus. Consider this an opportunity to learn together how to combine rest with abiding in him, and seek to accomplish this in ways that are practical and attainable, like taking time away from technology or waking up earlier.

Youth often goes hand-in-hand with impatience. It is just hard to wait for people, food we crave, an appointment, the end of the day, or the homecoming of a loved one. Our daughters are growing up in a society of instant gratification. Slowing the world down is not an option. What we *can* do is take them by the hand and hear the words of Psalm 119:103 together: "How sweet are your words to my taste, sweeter than honey to my mouth!"

The act of savouring the words of the psalmist invites us to slow down and abide. It is hard to enjoy a freshly baked chocolate chip cookie if we eat it all in one bite! And so it is with reading the Bible. We can read one verse at a time, underline it, talk about it, savour it. "You are my refuge and my shield; I have put my hope in your word" (Psalm 119:114). Slowing down to enjoy his word is a form of resting.

Sometimes we need to hide away in his word and let it surround and shield us. When days turn into weeks and we begin to sense that we are feeling weak and distant from God, we need more than ever to be held. "Uphold me, and I will be delivered" (Psalm 119:117).

What better way for our daughters to see our need for rest than when we acknowledge our busyness with life and how beautiful it is to sit at his feet and hear his gentle whisper as Elijah did: "After the earthquake came a fire, but the LORD was not in the fire. And after the fire came a gentle whisper" (1 Kings 19:12). My sister allowed me to find much needed refreshment from the demands of five children through precious cousin time, and this gave me strength.

Conversations and Connections with Your Daughter

WEEK 3

Day 1

Read Psalm 119:81–88.

** כ Kaph**
81 My soul faints with longing for your salvation,
but I have put my hope in your word.
82 My eyes fail, looking for your promise;
I say, "When will you comfort me?"
83 Though I am like a wineskin in the smoke,
I do not forget your decrees.
84 How long must your servant wait?
When will you punish my persecutors?
85 The arrogant dig pits to trap me,
contrary to your law.
86 All your commands are trustworthy;
help me, for I am being persecuted without cause.
87 They almost wiped me from the earth,
but I have not forsaken your precepts.
88 In your unfailing love preserve my life,
that I may obey the statutes of your mouth.

Highlight words or phrases that create a sense of how you can abide in God. Discuss the phrases *longing, hope in your word, comfort, I do not forget, your commands are trustworthy,* and *unfailing love.* What do these phrases mean for your daily walk with God? Consider ways to hope in his word.

Today's Key Verse
"My soul faints with longing for your salvation, but I have put my hope in your word" (Psalm 119:81).

Pray Together
Pray that you would rest in God's unfailing love.

Memorize the Weekly Verse
"Your word is a lamp for my feet, a light on my path" (Psalm 119:105).

Shared Journal Experience

Turn to the journal section for week 3, day 1, and switch back and forth, sharing words of encouragement.

Read Psalm 119:89–96.

ל Lamedh

⁸⁹ Your word, LORD, is eternal;
it stands firm in the heavens.
⁹⁰ Your faithfulness continues through all generations;
you established the earth, and it endures.
⁹¹ Your laws endure to this day,
for all things serve you.
⁹² If your law had not been my delight,
I would have perished in my affliction.
⁹³ I will never forget your precepts,
for by them you have preserved my life.
⁹⁴ Save me, for I am yours;
I have sought out your precepts.
⁹⁵ The wicked are waiting to destroy me,
but I will ponder your statutes.
⁹⁶ To all perfection I see a limit,
but your commands are boundless.

Highlight words or phrases that create a sense of how you can abide in God. Discuss the phrases *eternal*, *stands firm, faithfulness, you established the earth, I will never forget, save me, ponder your statutes,* and *your commands are boundless.* What do these phrases mean for your daily walk with God? Consider ways to be faithful.

Today's Key Verse

"Your faithfulness continues through all generations; you established the earth, and it endures" (Psalm 119:90).

Pray Together

Pray that God's law would be your delight and that you would be faithful, stand firm, and not forget his precepts.

Memorize the Weekly Verse

"Your word is a lamp for my feet, a light on my path" (Psalm 119:105).

Shared Journal Experience

Turn to the journal section for week 3, day 2, and switch back and forth, sharing words of encouragement.

Day 3

Read Psalm 119:97–104.

מ Mem

⁹⁷ Oh, how I love your law!
I meditate on it all day long.
⁹⁸ Your commands are always with me
and make me wiser than my enemies.
⁹⁹ I have more insight than all my teachers,
for I meditate on your statutes.
¹⁰⁰ I have more understanding than the elders,
for I obey your precepts.
¹⁰¹ I have kept my feet from every evil path
so that I might obey your word.
¹⁰² I have not departed from your laws,
for you yourself have taught me.
¹⁰³ How sweet are your words to my taste,
sweeter than honey to my mouth!
¹⁰⁴ I gain understanding from your precepts;
therefore I hate every wrong path.

Highlight words or phrases that create a sense of how you can abide in God. Discuss the phrases *love your law*, *meditate, commands are always with me, more understanding*, *kept my feet from every evil path*, *not departed*, and *sweet are your words*. What do these phrases mean for your daily walk with God? Consider ways to let God's word light your daily path.

Today's Key Verse

"Your commands are always with me and make me wiser than my enemies" (Psalm 119:98).

Pray Together

Pray that God's words would be sweeter than honey to your mouth.

Memorize the Weekly Verse

"Your word is a lamp for my feet, a light on my path" (Psalm 119:105).

Shared Journal Experience

Turn to the journal section for week 3, day 3, and switch back and forth, sharing words of encouragement.

Day 4

Read Psalm 119:105–112.

נ Nun
105 Your word is a lamp for my feet,
a light on my path.
106 I have taken an oath and confirmed it,
that I will follow your righteous laws.
107 I have suffered much;
preserve my life, LORD, according to your word.
108 Accept, LORD, the willing praise of my mouth,
and teach me your laws.
109 Though I constantly take my life in my hands,
I will not forget your law.
110 The wicked have set a snare for me,
but I have not strayed from your precepts.
111 Your statutes are my heritage forever;
they are the joy of my heart.
112 My heart is set on keeping your decrees
to the very end.

Highlight words or phrases that create a sense of how you can abide in God. Discuss the phrases *lamp for my feet, path, follow your righteous laws, preserve my life, praise of my mouth, teach me, heritage forever*, and *joy of my heart*. What do these phrases mean for your daily walk with God? Consider ways to set your heart on God's word.

Today's Key Verse

"Your statutes are my heritage forever; they are the joy of my heart" (Psalm 119:111).

Pray Together

Pray that you would remember God's statutes and that they would be the joy of your heart.

Memorize the Weekly Verse

"Your word is a lamp for my feet, a light on my path" (Psalm 119:105).

Shared Journal Experience

Turn to the journal section for week 3, day 4, and switch back and forth, sharing words of encouragement.

Read Psalm 119:113–120.

◖ Samekh

113 I hate double-minded people,
but I love your law.
114 You are my refuge and my shield;
I have put my hope in your word.
115 Away from me, you evildoers,
that I may keep the commands of my God!
116 Sustain me, my God, according to your promise, and I will live;
do not let my hopes be dashed.
117 Uphold me, and I will be delivered;
I will always have regard for your decrees.
118 You reject all who stray from your decrees,
for their delusions come to nothing.
119 All the wicked of the earth you discard like dross;
therefore I love your statutes.
120 My flesh trembles in fear of you;
I stand in awe of your laws.

Highlight words or phrases that create a sense of how you can abide in God. Discuss the phrases *love your law, refuge, my shield, put my hope, sustain me, your promise, uphold me,* and *I stand in awe*. What do these phrases mean for your daily walk with God? Consider ways to live according to the promises of God.

Today's Key Verse

"You are my refuge and my shield; I have put my hope in your word" (Psalm 119:114).

Pray Together

Pray that you would stand in awe of God's laws and put your hope in his word.

Memorize the Weekly Verse

"Your word is a lamp for my feet, a light on my path" (Psalm 119:105).

Shared Journal Experience

Turn to the journal section for week 3, day 5, and switch back and forth, sharing words of encouragement.

Consider supporting a child in need through an organization of your choice, and write a letter to the child.

Find restful activities to do together that you both enjoy. Take turns selecting one, such as hiking, art, a movie date, baking, or listening to music.

Worship together with these songs as you reflect on abiding in God's presence.

"Abide" (We Are Messengers)

"Thy Word" (Amy Grant)

"Abide with Me" (Matt Maher)

"Where My Hope Comes From" (Cliff Cline)

Closing Prayer for Week 3

Dear Lord, thank you that in your steadfast love we have life, and your word stands firm in the heavens. We can truly rest in the truth that you are faithful to all generations. Your word is a lamp for our feet, so guide us as we walk our paths. Forgive us, Lord, for allowing our lives to be so busy that we neglect to take the time to abide in your word. We need you, Lord. We don't want to forget your word, because it gives us life. Thank you for this time with my daughter, and thank you for teaching us through Psalm 119 that you are our refuge and shield. We stand in awe of you and love you. Amen.

WEEK 4
Listening and Living

Psalm 119:121–144
*Listening guides the soul of another towards a beautiful discovery
of resting in being heard.*

Memory Verse
"The unfolding of your words gives light; it gives understanding to the simple."
Psalm 119:130

Dear Moms

There is such strength in this verse. The unfolding of God's words gives us knowledge. Listening to him illuminates our path. Girls growing up in this generation *need* a good listener. Her friends can listen, but the gift we have as mothers is the ability to be her *first* best listener. I say with all honesty that I myself can be too quick to speak and too slow to listen. Sometimes I wish I could go back and just sit down, take a deep breath, and hear the heart that comes through the personal stories of my daughters. To fully absorb their facial expressions, tears, giggles, the rolling of eyes, the flicking of hair, and the understanding of what all those unconscious gestures actually mean. It is a challenge to reach the fullness and depth of that understanding. It takes time and practice—a habit worth aiming towards.

The phrase "I wish I had listened" rings through my mind when I reflect on moments when I chose to let my own way rule over my mother's way. When I was young and fearless in my determination to show off a new skill that I was so very proud of, I hurriedly grabbed my sparkling purple bike to show my best friend that I could go down a hill with no hands on the handlebars. You can imagine the disaster that followed: somersault over the handlebars, face-first at the bottom of the hill, much closer to the pavement than one would ever choose. Miraculously, I was not rushed to the emergency room, nor did I lose my front teeth, but I do remember a very swollen lip to match my bruised ego. I knew immediately that I should have listened to my mother's warnings about bike safety.

Sometimes, we have simple ways, and we need wise guidance. As the psalmist acknowledges, "I am your servant; give me discernment" (119:125). God is the ultimate "best" listener. The psalmist is crying out throughout Psalm 119, and God hears him, every single word. Isn't that beautiful? God knows what will be said before it is spoken (Psalm 139:4). We don't know what's going on in our daughter's mind or heart, but the gift God gives us is that we can rest in the truth that he knows.

Living a life that is full of gracious listening requires a discipline that can only come with practice. Our daughters need to be taught how to do this in order to grow up as stewards of each other and of their own daughters someday. They should know that living a life listening to God is sometimes just hard! But the hope is that together we can pray "Direct my footsteps according to your word; let no sin rule over me" (Psalm 119:133).

Our daughters will go over the handlebars of life at some point. Our challenge is to be there to listen when they do, while holding out our arms to comfort them and demonstrate God's unconditional love: "My command is this: Love each other as I have loved you" (John 15:12).

Conversations and Connections with Your Daughter

WEEK 4

Read Psalm 119:121–124.

ע Ayin
121 I have done what is righteous and just;
do not leave me to my oppressors.
122 Ensure your servant's well-being;
do not let the arrogant oppress me.
123 My eyes fail, looking for your salvation,
looking for your righteous promise.
124 Deal with your servant according to your love
and teach me your decrees.

Highlight words or phrases that create a sense of how you can live your life for God and listen to his instructions. Discuss the phrases *righteous, just, servant's well-being, my eyes fail, salvation, promise, according to your love,* and *teach me.* What do these phrases mean for your daily walk with God? Consider ways you can be discerning.

Today's Key Verse

"I am your servant; give me discernment that I may understand your statutes" (Psalm 119:125).

Pray Together

Pray for daily discernment.

Memorize the Weekly Verse

"The unfolding of your words gives light; it gives understanding to the simple" (Psalm 119:130).

Shared Journal Experience

Turn to the journal section for week 4, day 1, and switch back and forth, sharing words of encouragement.

Read Psalm 119:125–128.

[125] I am your servant; give me discernment
that I may understand your statutes.
[126] It is time for you to act, LORD;
your law is being broken.
[127] Because I love your commands
more than gold, more than pure gold,
[128] and because I consider all your precepts right,
I hate every wrong path.

Highlight words or phrases that create a sense of how you can live your life for God and listen to his instructions. Discuss the phrases *your servant, discernment, love your commands,* and *I hate every wrong path.* What do these phrases mean to your daily walk with God? Consider ways to love his commands and stay on the right path.

Today's Key Verse

"It is time for you to act, LORD; your law is being broken" (Psalm 119:126).

Pray Together

Pray that you would love his commands more than gold.

Memorize the Weekly Verse

"The unfolding of your words gives light; it gives understanding to the simple" (Psalm 119:130).

Shared Journal Experience

Turn to the journal section for week 4, day 2, and switch back and forth, sharing words of encouragement.

Day 3

Read Psalm 119:129–136.

ℸ **Pe**

129 Your statutes are wonderful;
therefore I obey them.
130 The unfolding of your words gives light;
it gives understanding to the simple.
131 I open my mouth and pant,
longing for your commands.
132 Turn to me and have mercy on me,
as you always do to those who love your name.
133 Direct my footsteps according to your word;
let no sin rule over me.
134 Redeem me from human oppression,
that I may obey your precepts.
135 Make your face shine on your servant
and teach me your decrees.
136 Streams of tears flow from my eyes,
for your law is not obeyed.

Highlight words or phrases that create a sense of how you can live your life for God and listen to his instructions. Discuss the phrases *your statutes are wonderful, words gives light, understanding, longing, turn to me, have mercy, direct my footsteps, no sin rule over me,* and *tears flow from my eyes.* What do these phrases mean for your daily walk with God? Consider the ways God's word gives light to the simple and how you can live according to his word.

Today's Key Verse

"Streams of tears flow from my eyes, for your law is not obeyed" (Psalm 119:136).

Pray Together

Pray that you would live according to God's word.

Memorize the Weekly Verse

"The unfolding of your words gives light; it gives understanding to the simple" (Psalm 119:130).

Shared Journal Experience

Turn to the journal section for week 4, day 3, and switch back and forth, sharing words of encouragement.

Read Psalm 119:137–140.

צ Tsadhe

[137] You are righteous, LORD,
and your laws are right.
[138] The statutes you have laid down are righteous;
they are fully trustworthy.
[139] My zeal wears me out,
for my enemies ignore your words.
[140] Your promises have been thoroughly tested,
and your servant loves them.

Highlight words or phrases that create a sense of how you can live your life for God and listen to his instructions. Discuss the phrases *righteous, laws are right, fully trustworthy, promises,* and *your servant loves them.* What do these phrases mean for your daily walk with God? Consider the ways you can fully trust God's statutes and love his promises.

Today's Key Verse

"Your promises have been thoroughly tested, and your servant loves them" (Psalm 110:140).

Pray Together

Pray that you would love God's promises.

Memorize the Weekly Verse

"The unfolding of your words gives light; it gives understanding to the simple" (Psalm 119:130).

Shared Journal Experience

Turn to the journal section for week 4, day 4 and switch back and forth sharing words of encouragement.

Day 5

Read Psalm 119:141–144.

¹⁴¹ Though I am lowly and despised,
I do not forget your precepts.
¹⁴² Your righteousness is everlasting
and your law is true.
¹⁴³ Trouble and distress have come upon me,
but your commands give me delight.
¹⁴⁴ Your statutes are always righteous;
give me understanding that I may live.

Highlight words or phrases that create a sense of how you can live your life for God and listen to his instructions. Discuss the phrases *I do not forget, everlasting, law is true, trouble and distress, your commands give me delight, always righteous,* and *understanding.* What do these phrases mean for your daily walk with God? Consider ways that even through trouble and distress you see his commands as a delight.

Today's Key Verse

"Trouble and distress have come upon me, but your commands give me delight" (Psalm 119:143).

Pray Together

Pray that you will delight in God's commands.

Memorize the Weekly Verse

"The unfolding of your words gives light; it gives understanding to the simple" (Psalm 119:130).

Shared Journal Experience

Turn to the journal section for week 4, day 5, and switch back and forth, sharing words of encouragement.

Write a note of encouragement to someone experiencing a difficult time. Surprise a neighbour or a friend with an invitation to dinner.

Worship together with these songs as you listen to God's voice in your life.

"Who You Say I Am" (Hillsong Worship)

"Yet Not I But Through Christ In Me" (CityAlight)

"I'm Listening" (Chris McClarney, featuring Hollyn)

"Living Hope" (Phil Wickham)

Closing Prayer for Week 4

Dear Lord, thank you for your presence in times of trouble and for the knowledge that we can call on you. Your commands give us delight and show us how to walk with you daily. Help us, Lord, to call on you with the knowledge that you will save us. Thank you that you hear our voices and that you are near to us. As we read more of your word, show us that it is truth and that you are forever. Amen.

WEEK 5
Managing Moments

Psalm 119:145-176

Let your day be more than just moment-to-moment. Let it be grand steps towards blessing upon blessing for others.

Memory Verse

"Great peace have those who love your law, and nothing can make them stumble."

Psalm 119:165

Dear Moms

Spontaneity is often thought of as impractical. But what if you could take a moment while still being purposeful? It may call for some preplanning and brainstorming, but the end is so worth the means. The pleasant surprise of a spontaneous moment that is managed well can turn into a memorable blessing.

Typically, after church on the average Sunday, you can hear the rumbles of hunger ripple loudly through the car on the ride home in any given family. The decision to stop for food is met with bursts of joy. Though it seems spontaneous to the children, it's planned ahead by their parents to provide a moment that becomes special to the whole family.

My parents often did this. Growing up, our surprise Sunday food was a KFC bucket of chicken. I remember squirming excitedly in my seat as we made our detour on the way home from church, hardly being able to handle the anticipated aroma of fried chicken just waiting to be devoured. It was the change in the ordinary coupled with the simple idea of being able to transform an otherwise mundane activity—a car ride home—into a moment of delicious fun and surprise.

Creating moments of spontaneity like this may not come naturally to you. It does to very few of us. Children tend to do it more naturally than we do, which is a good opportunity for us to listen well. Look ahead to your week or month for moments to briefly shake up your daughter's routine and surprise her. Her days are already written, as are yours. The beauty is that you *get* to be a part of her life, just as Psalm 139:16 says: "Your eyes saw my unformed body; all the days ordained for me were written in your book before one of them came to be."

I recall the time when my mom somehow knew that I needed an afternoon away from school. Perhaps it was motherly intuition, perhaps guidance from God; likely it was a combination of the two! Just when I needed it most, she turned the ordinary into the extraordinary, picked me up from school, and whisked me away for an afternoon adventure. I was blessed with a new pair of shoes I had longed for and had my ears pierced, but most importantly, I got to spend time with my mom, just the two of us. Anyone who grew up with siblings understands how special those moments are!

Not knowing until much later the extent of the planning and forethought my mom put into our little adventure is part of what makes it such a treasured memory. It shows how attentive Mom was to the needs of her children and that she was able to overcome any hurdles in order to so beautifully meet them. For that, I am forever grateful. Let's all dive into the little moments and make them amazing.

Conversations and Connections with Your Daughter

WEEK 5

Day 1

Read Psalm 119:145–152.

ק Qoph
145 I call with all my heart; answer me, LORD,
and I will obey your decrees.
146 I call out to you; save me
and I will keep your statutes.
147 I rise before dawn and cry for help;
I have put my hope in your word.
148 My eyes stay open through the watches of the night,
that I may meditate on your promises.
149 Hear my voice in accordance with your love;
preserve my life, LORD, according to your laws.
150 Those who devise wicked schemes are near,
but they are far from your law.
151 Yet you are near, LORD,
and all your commands are true.
152 Long ago I learned from your statutes
that you established them to last forever.

Highlight words or phrases that create a sense of how you can manage your moments and honour God. Discuss the phrases *with all my heart, I call out to you, I rise before dawn, hope in your word, eyes stay open, meditate on your promises, hear my voice, preserve my life, yet you are near,* and *I learned*. What do these phrases mean for your daily walk with God? Consider the ways you can draw near to God.

Today's Key Verse

"Yet you are near, LORD, and all your commands are true" (Psalm 119:151).

Pray Together

Pray for God to help you to know he is near every moment.

Memorize the Weekly Verse

"Great peace have those who love your law, and nothing can make them stumble" (Psalm 119:165).

Shared Journal Experience

Turn to the journal section for week 5, day 1, and switch back and forth, sharing words of encouragement.

Day 2

Read Psalm 119:153–156.

ר Resh

[153] Look on my suffering and deliver me,
for I have not forgotten your law.
[154] Defend my cause and redeem me;
preserve my life according to your promise.
[155] Salvation is far from the wicked,
for they do not seek out your decrees.
[156] Your compassion, LORD, is great;
preserve my life according to your laws.

Highlight words or phrases that create a sense of how you can manage your moments and honour God. Discuss the phrases *deliver me, not forgotten your law, redeem me, preserve my life,* and *your compassion, LORD, is great.* What do these phrases mean for your daily walk with God? Consider ways you can share how great his compassion is in your life.

Today's Key Verse

"Your compassion, LORD, is great; preserve my life according to your laws" (Psalm 119:156).

Pray Together

Pray that you would be compassionate toward others.

Memorize the Weekly Verse

"Great peace have those who love your law, and nothing can make them stumble" (Psalm 119:165).

Shared Journal Experience

Turn to the journal section for week 5, day 2, and switch back and forth, sharing words of encouragement.

Day 3

Read Psalm 119:157–160.

¹⁵⁷ Many are the foes who persecute me,
but I have not turned from your statutes.
¹⁵⁸ I look on the faithless with loathing,
for they do not obey your word.
¹⁵⁹ See how I love your precepts;
preserve my life, LORD, in accordance with your love.
¹⁶⁰ All your words are true;
all your righteous laws are eternal.

Highlight words or phrases that create a sense of how you can manage your moments and honour God. Discuss the phrases *but I have not turned, I love your precepts, preserve my life, with your love,* and *all your words are true.* What do these phrases mean for your daily walk with God? Consider the ways his word is true.

Today's Key Verse

"All your words are true; all your righteous laws are eternal" (Psalm 119:160).

Pray Together

Pray that you would believe the truth of God's word instead of lies.

Memorize the Weekly Verse

"Great peace have those who love your law, and nothing can make them stumble" (Psalm 119:165).

Shared Journal Experience

Turn to the journal section for week 5, day 3, and switch back and forth, sharing words of encouragement.

Day 4

Read Psalm 119:161–168.

ש Sin and Shin

161 Rulers persecute me without cause,
but my heart trembles at your word.
162 I rejoice in your promise
like one who finds great spoil.
163 I hate and detest falsehood
but I love your law.
164 Seven times a day I praise you
for your righteous laws.
165 Great peace have those who love your law,
and nothing can make them stumble.
166 I wait for your salvation, LORD,
and I follow your commands.
167 I obey your statutes,
for I love them greatly.
168 I obey your precepts and your statutes,
for all my ways are known to you.

Highlight words or phrases that create a sense of how you can manage your moments and honour God. Discuss the phrases *heart trembles at your word, rejoice in your promise, detest falsehood, love your law, seven times a day, great peace, I wait for your salvation, I love them greatly,* and *all my ways are known to you.* What do these phrases mean for our daily walk with God? Consider the ways God gives you peace.

Today's Key Verse

"I rejoice in your promise like the one who finds great spoil" (Psalm 119:162).

Pray Together

Pray that you would rejoice in God's promises.

Memorize the Weekly Verse

"Great peace have those who love your law, and nothing can make them stumble" (Psalm 119:165).

Shared Journal Experience

Turn to the journal section for week 5, day 4, and switch back and forth, sharing words of encouragement.

Congratulations, you have almost completed five weeks of time with your daughter discovering together the word of God through Psalm 119!

Read Psalm 119:169–176.

ת Taw

169 May my cry come before you, Lᴏʀᴅ;
give me understanding according to your word.
170 May my supplication come before you;
deliver me according to your promise.
171 May my lips overflow with praise,
for you teach me your decrees.
172 May my tongue sing of your word,
for all your commands are righteous.
173 May your hand be ready to help me,
for I have chosen your precepts.
174 I long for your salvation, Lᴏʀᴅ,
and your law gives me delight.
175 Let me live that I may praise you,
and may your laws sustain me.
176 I have strayed like a lost sheep.
Seek your servant,
for I have not forgotten your commands.

Highlight words or phrases that create a sense of how you can manage your moments and honour God. Discuss the phrases *may my cry come before you*, *give me understanding, deliver me, lips overflow with praise, sing of your word, long for salvation,* and *let me live that I may praise you.* What do these phrases mean for your daily walk with God? Consider ways you can stay close to God and not stray like lost sheep.

Today's Key Verse

"May my tongue sing of your word, for all your commands are righteous" (Psalm 119:172).

Pray Together

Pray that your words would overflow with praise for God.

Memorize the Weekly Verse

"Great peace have those who love your law, and nothing can make them stumble" (Psalm 119:165).

Shared Journal Experience

Turn to the journal section for week 5, day 5, and switch back and forth, sharing words of encouragement.

Send a copy of the lyrics of the song you chose in the shared journal entry on week 5, day 5, as an encouragement to a friend or family member. Create a place in your home that is intended for quiet, peaceful moments. Get creative together.

Worship together with these songs as you reflect on God's blessings in your life.

"We Turn Our Eyes" (Jeremy Camp and Adrienne Camp)

"My Lighthouse" (Rend Collective)

"Yes I Will" (Vertical Worship)

"Miracle of the Moment" (Steven Curtis Chapman)

Closing Prayer for Week 5

Dear Lord, we rejoice in your word and love your law. There is so much to learn, and we are so thankful that you give us understanding about your word. We want to praise you and sing praises, for your commandments are right! We need your hand to help us because we know that like sheep we are lost and need to seek you. Thank you for giving us your word; it is life to us! Amen.

Shared Journal Experience

The Switch

Write a word; inspire her heart.

Shared Journal Experience

Journaling back and forth with each other is a special way to communicate together. My hope is that you will look back on this unique experience with sweet memories of a close relationship with one another and ultimately a deeper understanding of how to study God's word, one verse at a time. May you continue to write a word and inspire her heart!

WEEK 1: DAY 1

Write the start date of your journey: _____.

Read Psalm 119:1–8.

Mom

Write out a verse for your daughter that stands out to you. What do you hope for on this journey?

_____

_____

_____

_____

_____

_____

_____

_____

_____

_____

_____

_____

_____

_____

_____

_____

_____

_____

_____

_____

_____

_____

Share a word with your mom to encourage her today. What do you hope for on this journey?

_____

_____

_____

_____

_____

_____

_____

_____

_____

_____

_____

_____

_____

_____

_____

_____

_____

_____

_____

_____

_____

_____

_____

_____

_____

_____

"Blessed are those who keep his statutes
and seek him with all their heart."

Psalm 119:2

WEEK 1: DAY 2

Read Psalm 119:9–16.

Mom

Write a keyword from today's verse and share with your daughter why you chose it.

_____

_____

_____

_____

_____

_____

_____

_____

_____

_____

_____

_____

_____

_____

_____

_____

_____

_____

_____

_____

_____

_____

_____

_____

Daughter

Write a keyword from the verse today and share with your mom why you chose it.

_____

_____

_____

_____

_____

_____

_____

_____

_____

_____

_____

_____

_____

_____

_____

_____

_____

_____

_____

_____

_____

_____

_____

_____

_____

_____

_____

_____

_____

_____

"I have hidden your word in my heart that I might not sin against you."

Psalm 119:11

WEEK 1: DAY 3

Read Psalm 119:17–24.

Mom

What inspires you about your daughter?

_____

_____

_____

_____

_____

_____

_____

_____

_____

_____

_____

_____

_____

_____

_____

_____

_____

_____

_____

_____

_____

_____

_____

_____

Daughter

Tell your mom how she inspires you.

_____

_____

_____

_____

_____

_____

_____

_____

_____

_____

_____

_____

_____

_____

_____

_____

_____

_____

_____

_____

_____

_____

_____

_____

_____

_____

_____

"Your statutes are my delight; they are my counselors."

Psalm 119:24

WEEK 1: DAY 4

Read Psalm 119:25–32.

Mom

Share how your daughter delights you.

_____

_____

_____

_____

_____

_____

_____

_____

_____

_____

_____

_____

_____

_____

_____

_____

_____

_____

_____

_____

_____

_____

_____

_____

_____

_____

Daughter

Share how your mom delights you.

_____
_____
_____
_____
_____
_____
_____
_____
_____
_____
_____
_____
_____
_____
_____
_____
_____
_____
_____
_____
_____
_____
_____
_____

"I run in the path of your commands, for you have broadened my understanding."

Psalm 119:32

WEEK 1: DAY 5

Read Psalm 119:33–40.

Mom

Share with your daughter a time when you noticed her being selfless towards others.

_____
_____
_____
_____
_____
_____
_____
_____
_____
_____
_____
_____
_____
_____
_____
_____
_____
_____
_____
_____
_____
_____
_____
_____
_____

Daughter

Share how your mom has been selfless towards you.

_____

_____

_____

_____

_____

_____

_____

_____

_____

_____

_____

_____

_____

_____

_____

_____

_____

_____

_____

_____

_____

_____

_____

_____

_____

> _"Turn my heart toward your statutes and_
> _not toward selfish gain."_
>
> Psalm 119:36

WEEK 2: DAY 1

Read Psalm 119:41–48.

Mom

Write out a verse for your daughter that stands out to you.

_____

_____

_____

_____

_____

_____

_____

_____

_____

_____

_____

_____

_____

_____

_____

_____

_____

_____

_____

_____

_____

_____

_____

_____

_____

_____

_____

_____

Daughter

Share a word with your mom to encourage her today.

_____
_____
_____
_____
_____
_____
_____
_____
_____
_____
_____
_____
_____
_____
_____
_____
_____
_____
_____
_____
_____
_____
_____
_____

> *"I will walk about in freedom, for I have*
> *sought out your precepts."*
>
> *Psalm 119:45*

WEEK 2: DAY 2

Read Psalm 119:49–56.

Mom

Write a keyword from the verses today and share with your daughter.

_____

_____

_____

_____

_____

_____

_____

_____

_____

_____

_____

_____

_____

_____

_____

_____

_____

_____

_____

_____

_____

_____

_____

_____

_____

_____

Daughter

Write how your mom encourages you.

_____

_____

_____

_____

_____

_____

_____

_____

_____

_____

_____

_____

_____

_____

_____

_____

_____

_____

_____

_____

_____

_____

"Remember your word to your servant, for you have given me hope."

Psalm 119:49

WEEK 2: DAY 3

Read Psalm 119:57–64.

Mom

Share words of hope found in a special friendship.

_____

_____

_____

_____

_____

_____

_____

_____

_____

_____

_____

_____

_____

_____

_____

_____

_____

_____

_____

_____

_____

_____

_____

_____

_____

Daughter

Share how you can be a friend and how someone has been a friend to you.

_____

_____

_____

_____

_____

_____

_____

_____

_____

_____

_____

_____

_____

_____

_____

_____

_____

_____

_____

_____

_____

_____

_____

_____

> _"I am a friend to all who fear you, to all who follow your precepts."_
>
> Psalm 119:63

WEEK 2: DAY 4

Read Psalm 119:65–72.

Mom

Share how your daughter is more precious than gold.

_____

_____

_____

_____

_____

_____

_____

_____

_____

_____

_____

_____

_____

_____

_____

_____

_____

_____

_____

_____

_____

_____

_____

_____

_____

_____

_____

Daughter

Share about your favourite treat and ask your mom for a date to go out and enjoy it.

_____

_____

_____

_____

_____

_____

_____

_____

_____

_____

_____

_____

_____

_____

_____

_____

_____

_____

_____

_____

_____

_____

_____

_____

_____

_____

"The law from your mouth is more precious to me than thousands of pieces of silver and gold."

Psalm 119:72

WEEK 2: DAY 5

Read Psalm 119:73–80.

Mom

Share the impact of a promise from God in your life.

Daughter

Share how you can show love to your mom and family.

_____
_____
_____
_____
_____
_____
_____
_____
_____
_____
_____
_____
_____
_____
_____
_____
_____
_____
_____
_____
_____
_____
_____
_____

"May your unfailing love be my comfort,
according to your promise to your servant."

Psalm 119:76

WEEK 3: DAY 1

Read Psalm 119:81–88.

Mom

Share about a time when you put your hope in someone or something. How did that turn out?

_____

_____

_____

_____

_____

_____

_____

_____

_____

_____

_____

_____

_____

_____

_____

_____

_____

_____

_____

_____

_____

_____

_____

Daughter

Share a hope that you have.

_____

_____

_____

_____

_____

_____

_____

_____

_____

_____

_____

_____

_____

_____

_____

_____

_____

_____

_____

_____

_____

_____

_____

_____

> *"My soul faints with longing for your*
> *salvation, but I have put my hope*
> *in your word."*
>
> Psalm 119:81

WEEK 3: DAY 2

Read Psalm 119:89–96.

Mom

Share what faithfulness looks like to you. Think of a date to go on together and invite your daughter today.

_____

_____

_____

_____

_____

_____

_____

_____

_____

_____

_____

_____

_____

_____

_____

_____

_____

_____

_____

_____

_____

_____

_____

Daughter

Share about a faithful friend or family member who inspires you.

_____
_____
_____
_____
_____
_____
_____
_____
_____
_____
_____
_____
_____
_____
_____
_____
_____
_____
_____
_____
_____
_____
_____
_____
_____

"Your faithfulness continues through all generations; you established the earth, and it endures."

Psalm 119:90

WEEK 3: DAY 3

Read Psalm 119:97–104.

Mom

Share how to be wise when making decisions. Remind your daughter of a fun memory from when she was very young.

_____

_____

_____

_____

_____

_____

_____

_____

_____

_____

_____

_____

_____

_____

_____

_____

_____

_____

_____

_____

_____

_____

_____

Daughter

Write about a time you needed wisdom to make a decision. How has your mom been wise?

_____

_____

_____

_____

_____

_____

_____

_____

_____

_____

_____

_____

_____

_____

_____

_____

_____

_____

_____

_____

_____

_____

_____

_____

_____

> *"Your commands are always with me and make me wiser than my enemies."*
>
> *Psalm 119:98*

WEEK 3: DAY 4

Read Psalm 119:105–112.

Mom

Brainstorm ideas to serve others and give them a chance to rest as well. Share how your daughter brings joy to you.

_____

_____

_____

_____

_____

_____

_____

_____

_____

_____

_____

_____

_____

_____

_____

_____

_____

_____

_____

_____

_____

_____

_____

_____

_____

Daughter

What brings you joy?

_____

_____

_____

_____

_____

_____

_____

_____

_____

_____

_____

_____

_____

_____

_____

_____

_____

_____

_____

_____

_____

_____

_____

_____

_____

> *"Your statutes are my heritage forever; they
> are the joy of my heart."*
>
> *Psalm 119:111*

WEEK 3: DAY 5

Read Psalm 119:113–120.

Mom

Share a hope you have for your daughter.

_____

_____

_____

_____

_____

_____

_____

_____

_____

_____

_____

_____

_____

_____

_____

_____

_____

_____

_____

_____

_____

_____

_____

_____

_____

_____

Daughter

Share a hope you have with your mom.

_____

_____

_____

_____

_____

_____

_____

_____

_____

_____

_____

_____

_____

_____

_____

_____

_____

_____

_____

_____

_____

_____

_____

_____

_____

"You are my refuge and my shield; I have put my hope in your word."

Psalm 119:114

WEEK 4: DAY 1

Read Psalm 119:121–124.

Mom

Share a time when you understood God's word in a new way.

_____

_____

_____

_____

_____

_____

_____

_____

_____

_____

_____

_____

_____

_____

_____

_____

_____

_____

_____

_____

_____

_____

_____

_____

_____

Daughter

Ask your mom a question about a favourite memory from when she was your age.

_____

_____

_____

_____

_____

_____

_____

_____

_____

_____

_____

_____

_____

_____

_____

_____

_____

_____

_____

_____

_____

_____

_____

*"I am your servant; give me discernment
that I may understand your statutes."*

Psalm 119:125

WEEK 4: DAY 2

Read Psalm 119:125–128.

Mom

Have you ever asked God to act? Share a time God acted for you.

Daughter

Share a time when someone acted with love towards you.

_____

_____

_____

_____

_____

_____

_____

_____

_____

_____

_____

_____

_____

_____

_____

_____

_____

_____

_____

_____

_____

_____

_____

"It is time for you to act, LORD; your law is being broken."

Psalm 119:126

WEEK 4: DAY 3

Read Psalm 119:129–136.

Mom

Share a time when you laughed so hard you cried and a time when you cried from sadness.

_____

_____

_____

_____

_____

_____

_____

_____

_____

_____

_____

_____

_____

_____

_____

_____

_____

_____

_____

_____

_____

_____

_____

_____

Daughter

Share what makes you laugh.

_____
_____
_____
_____
_____
_____
_____
_____
_____
_____
_____
_____
_____
_____
_____
_____
_____
_____
_____
_____
_____
_____

> _"Streams of tears flow from my eyes, for your law is not obeyed."_
>
> Psalm 119:136

WEEK 4: DAY 4

Read Psalm 119:137–140.

Mom

Share a time when your faith was tested and how you overcame the trial.

_____

_____

_____

_____

_____

_____

_____

_____

_____

_____

_____

_____

_____

_____

_____

_____

_____

_____

_____

_____

_____

_____

_____

_____

Daughter

Share about a hard time you have had and how you made it through.

_____

_____

_____

_____

_____

_____

_____

_____

_____

_____

_____

_____

_____

_____

_____

_____

_____

_____

_____

_____

_____

_____

_____

"Your promises have been thoroughly tested, and your servant loves them."

Psalm 119:140

WEEK 4: DAY 5

Read Psalm 119:141–144.

Mom

Talk about a time when you faced trouble and how God provided.

_____

_____

_____

_____

_____

_____

_____

_____

_____

_____

_____

_____

_____

_____

_____

_____

_____

_____

_____

_____

_____

_____

_____

_____

_____

Daughter

Share how you have been helpful to someone else.

_____

_____

_____

_____

_____

_____

_____

_____

_____

_____

_____

_____

_____

_____

_____

_____

_____

_____

_____

_____

_____

_____

_____

_____

_____

_____

_____

_____

_____

_____

"Trouble and distress have come upon me, but your commands give me delight."

Psalm 119:143

WEEK 5: DAY 1

Read Psalm 119:145–152.

Mom

Talk about how you want to draw near to your daughter, and share some fun things you can do together.

_____

_____

_____

_____

_____

_____

_____

_____

_____

_____

_____

_____

_____

_____

_____

_____

_____

_____

_____

_____

_____

_____

_____

_____

Daughter

Make a list of some fun things you would like to do with your mom.

_____

_____

_____

_____

_____

_____

_____

_____

_____

_____

_____

_____

_____

_____

_____

_____

_____

_____

_____

_____

_____

_____

_____

_____

_____

_____

> *"Yet you are near, L*ORD*, and all your commands are true."*
>
> *Psalm 119:151*

WEEK 5: DAY 2

Read Psalm 119:153–156.

Mom

How have you been shown compassion? How have you seen your daughter show compassion?

_____

_____

_____

_____

_____

_____

_____

_____

_____

_____

_____

_____

_____

_____

_____

_____

_____

_____

_____

_____

_____

_____

_____

Daughter

Think of some words that would make someone smile!

_____

_____

_____

_____

_____

_____

_____

_____

_____

_____

_____

_____

_____

_____

_____

_____

_____

_____

_____

_____

_____

_____

_____

_____

_____

"Your compassion, LORD, is great; preserve my life according to your laws."

Psalm 119:156

WEEK 5: DAY 3

Read Psalm 119:157–160.

Mom

Share a special character trait that you see in your daughter.

_____

_____

_____

_____

_____

_____

_____

_____

_____

_____

_____

_____

_____

_____

_____

_____

_____

_____

_____

_____

_____

_____

Daughter

Share something special about your mom.

"All your words are true; all your righteous laws are eternal."

Psalm 119:160

WEEK 5: DAY 4

Read Psalm 119:161–168.

Mom

Share about a time of peace in your life. What brings you peace in your home?

_____

_____

_____

_____

_____

_____

_____

_____

_____

_____

_____

_____

_____

_____

_____

_____

_____

_____

_____

_____

_____

_____

_____

_____

Daughter

Tell your mom about a time when you felt peaceful.

_____
_____
_____
_____
_____
_____
_____
_____
_____
_____
_____
_____
_____
_____
_____
_____
_____
_____
_____
_____
_____
_____
_____

"I rejoice in your promise like the one who finds great spoil."

Psalm 119:162

WEEK 5: DAY 5

Write the end date of your journey: _____.

Read Psalm 119:169–176.

Mom

Write out the lyrics to a favourite worship song or hymn. Reflect on what you have learned on this journey with your daughter.

_____

_____

_____

_____

_____

_____

_____

_____

_____

_____

_____

_____

_____

_____

_____

_____

_____

_____

_____

_____

_____

_____

_____

_____

Daughter

Do you have a favourite song? Share it with your mom. Write out one thing you have learned on this journey with your mom. What was your favourite part?

_____

_____

_____

_____

_____

_____

_____

_____

_____

_____

_____

_____

_____

_____

_____

_____

_____

_____

_____

_____

_____

_____

_____

_____

_____

_____

"May my tongue sing of your word, for all your commands are righteous."

Psalm 119:172

APPENDIX I
Write Your Longest Prayer

You are so blessed to love your daughter and show her the goodness of God! Be encouraged that this is not the end. Truly, this is the start of cultivating a pattern of intentionality with your daughter through God's word. Once you have completed this five-week devotional together, keep the momentum flowing! Find another psalm or passage in the Bible, and utilize the *Conversations and Connections with Your Daughter* style. This can become a relational stepping stone that can beautifully strengthen your bond as mother and daughter. I know how quickly our girls become young women, so the memory of lingering discussion, prayer, and journaling will present you with moments to look back on with gratitude.

Perhaps it is time to write your own longest prayer, a Psalm 119 challenge! In your journal, write a prayer as an offering to God—and may God inspire your heart. Jesus is the radiance of the glory of God, and as we raise our daughters, may we look to him. He is our hope-filled presence!

APPENDIX II
Leading Your Daughter to Christ

The details are not completely clear, but what I do know is that I came to my parents at the age of 13 and expressed my desire to know that I was saved and to be baptized. I had been told that I asked Jesus into my heart at a young age, but this was a distant memory, and I wanted to be sure.

The salvation of your daughter is in God's perfect and capable hands. John 6:40 reminds us of this truth: "For my Father's will is that everyone who looks to the Son and believes in him shall have eternal life, and I will raise them up at the last day," and further on we read, "No one can come to me unless the Father who sent me draws them, and I will raise them up at the last day" (John 6:44). These verses are a reminder that we don't draw in our daughter; God does! With that reality, we have freedom to actively pray for her heart to be turned towards him, and for ourselves, we pray that we would rest in his sovereignty and with his help radiate Christ. It is the work of the Holy Spirit in her life that changes her heart. We diligently and consistently pray.

A great place to begin is with the fact that **we are all born sinners and in need of saving**. In Romans 3:10 we are told, "As it is written: 'There is no one righteous, not even one,'" and in Romans 3:23 we are reminded that "For all have sinned and fall short of the glory of God." We are sinners, separated from God, "But God demonstrates his own love for us in this: While we were still sinners, Christ died for us" (Romans 5:8). We help our daughter understand that her sin nature (the things she does such as lying, cheating, not honouring Mom and Dad, to name a few) keeps her from a relationship with a Holy God.

God sent his Son to save us from our sins, and John 3:16 beautifully announces this truth: "For God so loved the world that he gave his one and only

Son, that whoever believes in him shall not perish but have eternal life." He died in our place and rose again and is preparing a place for us. "My Father's house has many rooms; if that were not so, would I have told you that I am going there to prepare a place for you?" (John 14:2). When I was young, knowing that God was preparing a place for me was exciting. This personal perspective was comforting and provided me with hope and anticipation of what was to come. It is good to know these truths, but we have to receive and respond to Christ's invitation to be forgiven.

Receive the gift of salvation. Understanding our sin and knowing that God sent his Son to die on the cross in our place and rise again on the third day leads us into receiving Christ and trusting him to forgive our sins. It is a gift that we respond to and receive! "If you declare with your mouth, 'Jesus is Lord,' and believe in your heart that God raised him from the dead, you will be saved" (Romans 10:9). It is a gift God gives us: "For it is by grace you have been saved, through faith—and this is not from yourselves, it is the gift of God—not by works, so that no one can boast" (Ephesians 2:8–9).

If your daughter expresses a desire to receive Christ as her personal Saviour, you can share this prayer with her; it is a prayer similar to what I prayed many years ago: *Dear Jesus, I know that you died on the cross for my sins and rose again! I know that you love me and have a plan for my life. Today I receive your gift of eternal life and ask you to come into my heart and take the lead in my life. Amen.*

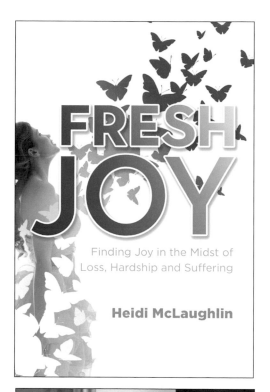

FRESH JOY

Finding Joy in the Midst of
Loss, Hardship and Suffering

Heidi McLaughlin

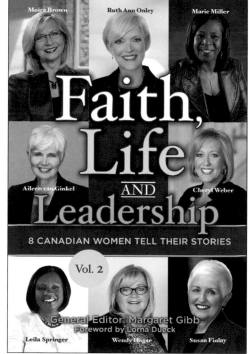

Moira Brown   Ruth Ann Onley   Marie Miller

Aileen van Ginkel   Cheryl Weber

Faith, Life AND Leadership

8 CANADIAN WOMEN TELL THEIR STORIES

Vol. 2

General Editor: Margaret Gibb
Foreword by Lorna Dueck

Leila Springer   Wendy Hagar   Susan Finlay